Farmer Flo's Happy Cows

Written by
Jill Atkins

Illustrated by
Leo Trinidad

It was time for milking on Hilltop Farm. Farmer Flo whizzed down on her quad bike.

"Oh no!" complained Moira. "I'm in a bad mood. I think I'll stay here."

"Come on, Moi," said Joy.

"But it's such a long way from Lower Bottom Field up to the milking shed," mooed Moira. "I'm not going."

All the other cows climbed up the hill and plodded along the lane to the milking shed.

Farmer Flo's boy, Paul, came to milk Moira.

"That's better," mooed Moira. "I'm in a good mood now."

The next day, Moira decided to stay in the field again.

"It's much better being milked here," she said.

"Well, I've got a bone in my leg," complained Joy. "So I'm not going up there today. I'm staying here with you."

"Come on, Moi," mooed Daisy. "And you too, Joy."

All the other cows climbed up the hill and along the lane to the milking shed.

Paul's sister, Hayley, joined him in the field. Paul and Hayley milked Moira and Joy.

The next day, Daisy refused to go too.

"I've got a hole in my hoof," she yawned. "And I'm worn out. It's my turn to stay here."

She was the third cow to complain. So little Royston came to milk her.

When the other cows came back from the milking shed, they were cross.

"It's not fair!" complained Jane.

"We want to be milked here too," said Doina.

They made some signs.

Moo! We shall not go up there!

Moo! We're staying here!

Moo! Down with the milking shed!

They sat down on the ground.

"We're staying here!" they chanted.

Farmer Flo frowned. She had no other children to milk the rest of the cows. What could she do?

She thought and thought. Then she said, "I know just what to do!"

The next day, the cows heard loud noises from the milking shed.

Crash! Boing! Whoop! Crunch! Rummm! Ping! Whizz! Zoing! Clang!

"What's going on?" they muttered to each other.

Suddenly, there was a growl and a clang. The cows huddled together in fright.

"Moo!" said Daisy.

"Moo!" said Moira.

"Mooooo!" said Joy.

The growling and clanging grew louder and louder.

"It's getting nearer!" said Moira.

"What is it?" asked Joy.

"It's a monster!" said Daisy.

"It's from outer space!" said Moira.

It was Farmer Flo!

"I like to have happy cows," she laughed. "If my cows won't come to the milking shed, I'll bring the milking shed to them!"

"Wow!" exclaimed Moira. "Thanks, Farmer Flo. Now we're very happy cows!"